# COMMAND *the* MORNING

## DAILY PRAYER MANUAL *for* BUSINESS OWNERS

JOHN MILLER

# COMMAND THE MORNING: DAILY PRAYER MANUAL FOR BUSINESS OWNERS

*by John Miller*



Published by One Life Books
Printed in the United States of America



All correspondences should be sent to
e-mail: johnmillerbooks@gmail.com

For more John Miller books visit,
www.johnmillerbooks.com

# CONTENTS

# DEDICATION

This book is dedicated to all business owners who desire to take charge of their day, profit in business and make it back home safe and sound everyday.

# BOOKS BY JOHN MILLER

## THE LIFE OF JESUS CHRIST SERIES

1. **The Last Week of Jesus Christ:** The Full Gospel Account of the Death, Resurrection & Ascension of Jesus Christ (Available in both text-only and illustrated editions)
2. **Jesus Christ the Healer:** The Full Gospel Account of the Healing Miracles of Jesus Christ (Available in both text-only and illustrated editions)
3. **Jesus Christ the Deliverer:** The Full Gospel Account of the Deliverance Ministrations of Jesus Christ (Available in both text-only and illustrated editions)
4. **Jesus Christ the Miracle Worker:** The Full Gospel Account of the Miracles of Jesus Christ (Available in both text-only and illustrated editions)
5. **Jesus Christ the Storyteller:** The Full Gospel Account of the Parables & Spiritual Illustrations of Jesus Christ (Available in both text-only and illustrated editions)

## COMMAND THE MORNING SERIES

1. Command the Morning: Daily Prayer Manual

2. Command the Morning: Daily Prayer Manual for Business Owners
3. Command the Morning: Daily Prayer Manual for Working People
4. Command the Morning: Daily Prayer Manual for Single Men
5. Command the Morning: Daily Prayer Manual for Single Women
6. Command the Morning: Daily Prayer Manual for Husbands and Fathers
7. Command the Morning: Daily Prayer Manual for Wives and Mothers
8. Command the Morning: Daily Prayer Manual for The Family
9. Command the Morning: Daily Prayer Manual for Students

**PRAY YOUR WAY SERIES**

1. Pray Your Way Into 2016
2. Pray Your Way Into 2016 for Single Men
3. Pray Your Way Into 2016 for Single Women
4. Pray Your Way Into 2016 for Married Men
5. Pray Your Way Into 2016 for Married Women
6. Pray Your Way Into 2016 for Students

**OPEN HEAVENS SERIES**

1. Open Heavens Prayers for Gainful Employment
2. Open Heavens Prayers for Fertility and Pregnancy

**PRAYER RAIN SERIES**

1. Prayer Rain: Powerful Prayers For Business Breakthrough
2. Prayer Rain: Breakthrough Prayers For Startups & Entrepreneurs
3. Prayer Rain: Breakthrough Prayers For Family-Sponsored Immigration & Permanent Residency
4. Prayer Rain: Breakthrough Prayers For Employment-Based Immigration & Permanent Residency
5. Prayer Rain: Breakthrough Prayers For Investment-Based Immigration & Permanent Residency

For newer books visit, www.johnmillerbooks.com

# INTRODUCTION

**If you want to fulfill destiny this year, please do not leave your house in the morning without using this book.**

I will introduce this devotional with the following essential scriptures:

Job 38:12 "***Have you commanded the morning*** since your days began, and caused the dawn to know its place..."

Mark 1:35-38, 40-42 "***Now in the morning, having risen a long while before daylight***, He (Jesus) went out and departed to a solitary place; ***and there He prayed***. And Simon and those who were with Him searched for Him. When they found Him, they said to Him, 'Everyone is looking for You.' But He said to them, 'Let us go into the next towns, that I may preach there also, ***because for this purpose*** I have come forth.' ... ***Now a leper came to Him***, imploring Him, kneeling down to Him and saying to Him, 'If You are willing, You can make me clean.' Then Jesus, moved with compassion, stretched out His hand and touched him, and said to him, ***'I am willing; be cleansed.'*** As soon as He had spoken, immediately the leprosy left him, and he was cleansed."

John 14:12-14 "Most assuredly, I say to you, he who believes in Me, the works that I do he will do also; and greater works than these he will do, because I go to My

Father. And whatever you ask in My name, that I will do, that the Father may be glorified in the Son. If you ask anything in My name, I will do it."

Here is the interpretation of all the above scriptures in plain english:

1. God Almighty issues commands to everything including the morning and the dawn. This was what He was telling Job in Job 38:12, amongst other things.

2. Jesus Christ, the Son of God, while on earth engaged in morning prayers. These morning prayers of Christ were without doubt focused on fulfilling His purpose.

3. Jesus Christ confirmed that His purpose on earth was to preach (the gospel, healing, deliverance, etc).

4. A few verses later, we see the immediate result of Christ's morning prayers. On the strength of that morning's prayers, he fulfilled His purpose for that day. Amongst other things, He physically touched a leprous man and instantly and completely healed him of the leprosy.

5. If you have discovered your purpose, you can do what Jesus Christ did and achieve greater results than He did because according to John 14:12-14, He has guaranteed to make this happen for you.

Jesus performed many miracles while He was on the earth because they were all part of His purpose.

Just like God spoke to Job about His use of commands, many of Christ's miracles were also achieved by commands. He would issue a command such as "Peace, Be Still" for example, and violent storms would seize. He commanded demons, the weather, animate and inanimate objects and everything obeyed Him. It is without doubt that many of these miracles He performed during the day had already been addressed in prayer, including His morning prayers. If this was not the case, then He would not have bothered to pray at all.

The world of business is a big battlefield. If you are a business owner, you know that everyday, business presents you with all sorts of battles. There are battles to create or stock desirable products or provide quality services, battles for customers, battles with competitors and so on. In order to succeed in business, you must fight and win these battles. In addition, you are a human being and as such you remain subject to all the battles every other human must face including the daily battle for your safety and health as well as battles against powers of darkness amongst others which will make serious effort to pull you down even this year.

To be a victor in business and in life and to become prosperous according to God's will, you need to master the spiritual tools that can help you achieve victory in all your daily battles. If this is your desire, "Command the Morning: Daily Prayer Manual for Business Owners" is a unique book that can help you. This prayer manual was written to enable you actualize what was promised to you in John 14:12-14, so that you can fulfill your purpose and destiny on earth just like Jesus did, using the same instruments He used - prayers and commands. What's more, this prayer manual also provides the essential bible passages, confessions, prayers and blessing with which to take complete charge of your day, therefore allowing you to achieve daily victory in business and in life.

That said, this book is not intended to replace any regular daily devotional book you might have gotten. You can use it together with any other material you already have. BUT if you desire to take full charge of your day, please do not leave your house in the morning without using this book. Without a doubt, if you do everything that is written in this book everyday and you have faith, you all will live a life of destiny fulfillment and achievement even as your life continues to please the Almighty.

Your friend-in-Christ,
John Miller

# HOW TO USE THIS BOOK

This book is unlike your regular daily devotional. It contains specific bible passages, praise and worship pieces, confessions, declarations and prayers which a business owner can use to take charge of the day. By carrying out the activities in this book, you will be able to successfully program your day and get the outcome that you desire.

This book is designed to be used in the sequence in which the content is presented. Thus, each morning, you need to go through page by page until you reach the final page.

The following are the relevant sections within the book for your daily use:

## THANK GOD, I AM ALIVE! (TGIAA)

1. Morning Words of Thanksgiving to God
2. Morning Words of Praise to God
3. Songs of Thanksgiving, Praise, Worship & Prayer

## ESSENTIAL DAILY PRAYERS

4. Bible Confessions & Readings
5. I Command Nature to Work In My Favor

## THEMATIC PRAYERS FOR BUSINESS OWNERS



## THE BLESSING

# YOU MUST BE BORN AGAIN

John 3:16 "For God so loved the world, that he gave his only begotten Son, that whosoever believeth in him should not perish, but have everlasting life." If you have not yet given your life to Jesus Christ, the prayers in this book will not work for you. The good news is that becoming born again is very simple. Simply read the words below within your mind, making sure to do this with full faith and belief in Jesus Christ. Thereafter, read these words out loud like a declaration or an acknowledgment of what you believe:

**"Lord Jesus, I believe that you are the Son of God. I believe that God sent you to the earth and gave you up to die for my sins. I also believe that God raised you from the dead. Today, I give my life to you for you to become the Lord of it. All my thoughts and deeds, I lay plain before you to be totally responsible for. You have said in your word that if I open the door of my life, you will come in. I open my heart to you and I invite you in to come and become the Lord of my life. Thank you for accepting me and giving me the assurance of eternal life."**

With those words spoken in your spirit and confessed with your mouth, you have given your life to Jesus Christ according to Romans 10:10 which says "For it is with your heart that you believe and are justified, and it is with your mouth that you profess your faith and are saved."

You are now what is known as a Born-again christian with full rights to the benefits of the kingdom of God.

# SECTION 1

# THANK GOD, I AM ALIVE!
# (TGIAA)

# 1

# MORNING WORDS OF THANKSGIVING TO GOD

1. Father, I thank you that I am alive!

2. Many who also slept yesterday are dead but I am alive. For this Lord, I thank you for the miracle of sleeping and waking up.

3. Father, I thank you for honoring my prayers of last night and for not allowing any evil to befall me in my sleep. I thank you for the battles that you fought for me during my sleep including those that I know about and those that I have no knowledge of.

4. Lord, I thank you for your hand of protection over my family throughout the night.

5. Lord, I thank you for protecting everything that I own and for not allowing me suffer any loss throughout the night.

6. Lord, I thank you for the dreams that you showed me during the night and for the instructions that you passed into my spirit to guide me today.

7. Lord, I thank you for loading me with today's benefits according to your word.

8. I thank you for your Power that can never fail.

9. Father, I thank you for sending your son, the Lord Jesus Christ, who has redeemed me from the fires of hell and given me the assurance of eternal life.

10. Thank you because you are my rock, my fortress and my deliverer. In you I take refuge. You are my shield and the horn of my salvation, my stronghold. I bless you.

# 2

# MORNING WORDS OF PRAISE TO GOD

1. This morning I declare that there is none like you O God.

2. Today, I declare that you alone are the King of Kings and Lord of Lords.

3. You are the I am that I am. Lord be lifted high and be glorified forever and ever.

4. Lord I bless you this morning even as the sun, moon and stars declare your glory.

5. This morning all of creation praises you, O Lord.

6. Father, I bow before you because you are Omnipotent, Omniscient and Omnipresent.

7. You are the Alpha and Omega - the beginning and the ending.

8. You are the One who is, the One who was, the One who is to come.

9. You are worthy to be called Wonderful Counselor, Mighty God, Everlasting Father and Prince of Peace.

10. You are worthy to be praised and you are worthy to be glorified. Lord, receive all my praises, glory, honor and adoration, in Jesus name.

# 3

# SONGS OF THANKSGIVING, PRAISE, WORSHIP & PRAYER

Video clips of these songs are available via the links provided below but you can also purchase them on Amazon, iTunes and other digital stores so that you have a permanent copy and listen on your device of choice wherever you are.

1. THANK YOU LORD
   For sing-along video and lyrics, see
   https://www.youtube.com/watch?v=K44trVhtZX4

2. GOD IS GOOD
   For sing-along video and lyrics, see
   https://www.youtube.com/watch?v=Jlo6RN5zRxk

3. GOD WILL MAKE A WAY WHERE THERE SEEMS TO BE NO WAY
   For sing-along video and lyrics, see
   https://www.youtube.com/watch?v=1z03fJYtS-0

4. NOTHING IS IMPOSSIBLE WITH GOD
   For sing-along video and lyrics, see
   https://www.youtube.com/watch?v=rips2XpzkjE

# SECTION 2

# DAILY READINGS, CONFESSIONS & PRAYERS

# 4

# BIBLE
# CONFESSIONS & READINGS

Take each of these scriptures and declare them out loud with complete faith in the Almighty.

**PSALM 121**

I will lift up mine eyes unto the hills, from whence cometh my help. My help cometh from the Lord, which made heaven and earth. He will not suffer my foot to be moved: He that keepeth me will not slumber.

Behold, He that keepeth Israel shall neither slumber nor sleep. The Lord is my keeper: the Lord is my shade upon my right hand.

The sun shall not smite me by day, nor the moon by night. The Lord shall preserve me from all evil: He shall preserve my soul. The Lord shall preserve my going out and my coming in from this time forth, and even forevermore. Amen.

**PSALM 23**

The Lord is my shepherd; I shall not want. He maketh me to lie down in green pastures: He leadeth me beside the still waters. He restoreth my soul: He leadeth me in the paths of righteousness for His name's sake.

Yea, though I walk through the valley of the shadow of death, I will fear no evil: for thou art with me; thy rod and thy staff they comfort me.

Thou preparest a table before me in the presence of mine enemies: thou anointest my head with oil; my cup runneth over. Surely goodness and mercy shall follow me all the days of my life: and I will dwell in the house of the Lord forever. Amen.

**PSALM 91**

I dwell in the secret place of the most High and I abide under the shadow of the Almighty. I will say of the Lord, He is my refuge and my fortress: my God; in Him will I trust.

Surely He shall deliver me from the snare of the fowler, and from the noisome pestilence. He shall cover me with his feathers, and under His wings shalt I trust: His truth shall be my shield and buckler. I shalt not be afraid for the terror by night; nor for the arrow that flieth by day; Nor for the pestilence that walketh in darkness; nor for the destruction that wasteth at noonday.

A thousand shall fall at my side, and ten thousand at my right hand; but it shall not come nigh me. Only with my eyes shalt I behold and see the reward of the wicked.

Because I have made the Lord, which is my refuge, even the most High, my habitation; There shall no evil befall me, neither shall any plague come nigh my dwelling. For He shall give his angels charge over me, to

keep me in all my ways. They shall bear me up in their hands, lest I dash my foot against a stone.
I shalt tread upon the lion and adder: the young lion and the dragon shalt I trample under feet.

Because I have set my love upon Him, therefore will He deliver me: He will set me on high, because I have known His name.

I shall call upon God, and He will answer me: He will be with me in trouble; He will deliver me, and honour me. With long life will He satisfy me, and shew me His salvation. Amen.

*If you have additional scriptures which you feel you need to declare, you can make the declarations now.*

# 5

# I COMMAND NATURE TO WORK IN MY FAVOR TODAY

You have the daily right and responsibility as a child of God to issue commands to nature, celestial bodies and all other elements of creation. If you exercise your right and command them (in accordance with God's will) to work in your favor, they will obey you. However, if you do not use your right, they will do nothing in your favor or worse, can work against you.

Joshua 10:12-13 "Then spake Joshua to the Lord in the day when the Lord delivered up the Amorites before the children of Israel, and he said in the sight of Israel, ***Sun, stand thou still upon Gibeon; and thou, Moon, in the valley of Ajalon***. And the sun stood still, and the moon stayed, until the people had avenged themselves upon their enemies. Is not this written in the book of Jasher? So the sun stood still in the midst of heaven, and hasted not to go down about a whole day."

Mark 4:38-41 "And He was in the hinder part of the ship, asleep on a pillow: and they awake Him, and say unto Him, Master, carest thou not that we perish? And He arose, and rebuked the wind, and said unto the sea, **Peace, be still**. And the wind ceased, and there was a great calm. And He said unto them, Why are ye so fearful? how is it that ye have no faith? And they feared exceedingly, and said one to another, ***What manner of man is this, that even the wind and the sea obey him?"***

John 14:12-14 "Most assuredly, I say to you, he who believes in Me, the works that I do he will do also; and greater works than these he will do, because I go to My Father. And whatever you ask in My name, that I will do, that the Father may be glorified in the Son. **If you ask anything in My name, I will do it.**"

Now, issue the following commands in accordance with your right as a child of God:

1. You the Stars in the firmament, you shall work in my favor today and you shall work against those who seek my hurt, in the name of Jesus.

2. You Moon, you shall work in my favor today and you shall work against those who seek my hurt, in the name of Jesus.

3. You Sun, you shall work in my favor today and you shall work against those who seek my hurt, in the name of Jesus.

4. You the Sky and the Clouds, you shall work in my favor today and you shall work against those who seek my hurt, in the name of Jesus.

5. You the Earth, you shall work in my favor today and you shall work against those who seek my hurt, in the name of Jesus.

6. You the Waters, you shall work in my favor today and you shall work against those who seek my hurt, in the name of Jesus.

7. You the Wind, you shall work in my favor today and you shall work against those who seek my hurt, in the name of Jesus.

8. You Fire, you shall work in my favor today and you shall work against those who seek my hurt, in the name of Jesus.

9. Today, I command every living creature made by God that flies in the air, that swims in the waters, that lives on the earth or within the earth to work in my favor and to work against those who seek my hurt, in the name of Jesus.

10. I command any weather that shall present itself today to work in my favor and work against all those who seek my hurt, in the name of Jesus.

# 6

# O GATES, OPEN UNTO ME

In the spirit realm, gates serve several crucial purposes. One of the most fundamental purposes of gates is to regulate access. Gates can allow things to come in, keep things in, allow things to go out or keep things out. Gates, for the most part, also work optimally at particular times of the day and in reaction to a necessity or demand placed on them.

An essential spiritual fact that we all need to understand is that everything that exists in the world has a gate, including you. You must issue commands to spiritual gates before you leave your house each morning so that you can maximize the day.

Isaiah 45:1-2 "Thus says the Lord to His anointed, To Cyrus, whose right hand I have held — To subdue nations before him And loose the armor of kings, ***to open before him the double doors, So that the gates will not be shut:*** 'I will go before you and make the crooked places straight; ***I will break in pieces the gates of bronze and cut the bars of iron."***

Isaiah 60:11 ***"Therefore Your gates shall be open continually;*** They shall not be shut day or night, ***That men may bring to you the wealth of the Gentiles***, And their kings in procession."

Acts 12:10 "They passed the first and second guards ***and came to the iron gate*** leading to the city. ***It opened***

***for them by itself, and they went through it."***

Now, issue the following commands in accordance with your right as a child of God:

1. O Gates of my life, I command you this morning, OPEN!, that the wealth of the gentiles can flow into you, in the name of Jesus.

2. O Gates of this day, OPEN unto me now, so that I can get the good that is in you, in the name of Jesus.

3. O Gates of my city, OPEN unto me now, so that I can enter into you and prosper within you, in the name of Jesus.

4. O Gates of my state, OPEN unto me now, so that I can enter into you and prosper within you, in the name of Jesus.

5. O Gates of my country, OPEN unto me now, so that I can enter into you and prosper within you, in the name of Jesus.

6. O Gates of the world, OPEN unto me now, so that I can enter into you and prosper within you, in the name of Jesus.

# 7

# PRAYERS AGAINST SPIRITUAL ATTACKS OF THE DAY

1. By the power in the name of Jesus, I spoil completely the consequence of any bad dream I had overnight. Nothing in it shall come to pass, in the name of Jesus.

2. Any object of darkness shot against my life in the night by powers of darkness for any reason and to achieve whatever purpose, right now, I command you, return to sender, in the name of Jesus.

3. I speak against any demonic plan of darkness which is meant to be executed upon my life today. Listen to me, I put a permanent stop to your execution and I command destruction upon you and your planners, in the name of Jesus.

4. As I go out today, I exercise the power given to me by the Lord Jesus Christ and I tread upon serpents and scorpions, and over all the power of the enemy fashioned against me. Nothing shall by any means hurt me, in the name of Jesus.

5. Today, I rededicate myself to the Lord Jesus Christ and I rekindle His Holy Spirit in my life with all the benefits, in the name of Jesus.

# 8

# PRAYERS AGAINST PHYSICAL ATTACKS OF THE DAY

1. O Lord my God, rise up for my sake and frustrate any plan of agents of darkness to take my life. I shall not die but live, in the name of Jesus.

2. My Father and my God, rise up for my sake and destroy any plan of darkness prepared to wound me and render me invalid, in the name of Jesus.

3. Almighty God, rise up for my sake and expose any plan of darkness fashioned to make me lose my source of income and the ability to make wealth, in the name of Jesus

4. Today, I speak against any agent of darkness issuing threats against my life. Lord, behold their threatenings, let all their threats against me be executed upon them, in the name of Jesus.

5. O Lord, you are my protector, protect me from any form of physical harm, in the name of Jesus.

*If you have the need and time this morning to address any other sort of physical attack peculiar to you, you can do that at this point.*

# 9

# O LORD, ORDER MY STEPS TODAY

Proverbs 16:9 "A man's heart plans his way, But the Lord directs his steps."

Psalm 119:133-136 "Direct my steps by Your word, And let no iniquity have dominion over me."

No matter how great you are, you need to ask for the direction and guidance of the Almighty so that you do not fall into error. No one follows God's direction and fails to fulfill destiny because God values His word above His own name.

1. My Lord and my God, as I go out today, have mercy upon me and order my steps, in the name of Jesus.

2. Almighty God, guide my thoughts and my deeds today so that I do not end up in the wrong place, at the wrong time doing the wrong thing, in the name of Jesus.

3. I withdraw my name from the roster of the victims of misfortune for today, in the name of Jesus.

4. O Lord today, send your angels out on assignment for my sake. Throughout this day, let them bear up my hands so that my feet of destiny will not strike against

the stone of misfortune, in the name of Jesus.

5. I decree into this day ahead of me: I shall go out and return home safely and I will not come across any misfortune and neither shall bad luck locate me, in the name of Jesus.

*If you have the need and time, feel free to add more prayers at this point.*

# 10

# PRAYERS AGAINST TEMPTATION & SIN

1. I decree this morning that I shall not commit any sin throughout the day that will lead to my death, in the name of Jesus.

2. I speak destruction to any habit or sin in my life which has become an access door of demons and infirmity into my life. As I abandon this sin today, I remove and block completely any entry door of evil into my life, in the name of Jesus.

3. You the voice of disgrace and downfall disguised in the form of sin and whispering evil thoughts into my mind, I command you to be silenced now, in the name of Jesus.

4. Most High God, cause any human agent of darkness, who has been a constant source of temptation and harassment to my life, to be removed from my vicinity today by any divine means necessary, in the name of Jesus.

5. Satan, I declare unto you today, I am for Christ and Christ alone. Get Thee Behind Me! I refuse to fall for any temptation you shall bring my way today, in the

name of Jesus.

*If you have the need and time, feel free to add more prayers at this point.*

# 11

# INTERCESSORY PRAYERS FOR FAMILY MEMBERS & OTHER LOVED ONES

Replace the gaps with the name of the loved one(s) you want to pray for today. Repeat as often as necessary.

1. Heavenly Father, as __________ goes out today, let _________ not be a victim of misfortune, in the name of Jesus.

2. Lord Jesus rise up for my sake and frustrate any plan of darkness that has been hatched against _________ . It shall not happen, in the name of Jesus.

3. Father, I decree favor upon __________'s life. Anywhere _________ goes today, let there be an outpouring of favor, in the name of Jesus.

4. Any sickness or disease in the life of __________ affecting ______'s quality of life and threatening to cut it short, hear me and hear me well, DIE NOW, in the name of Jesus.

5. I decree prosperity upon _________ . You shall not suffer loss today, in the name of Jesus.

# SECTION 3

# THEMATIC PRAYERS FOR BUSINESS OWNERS

# 12

# PRAYERS FOR GOOD HEALTH

1. My Father, my body is the temple of your Holy Spirit, drive out from it any sickness and disease, in the name of Jesus.

2. Lord God of heaven, I come before you today to ask for good health. Give it to me in the name of Jesus.

3. O Lord, create in me a merry heart that will fill me with divine medicine and remove from me any spirit of brokenness that will cause my bones to dry up, in the name of Jesus.

4. As I go out today, I receive divine immunization against any communicable disease, in the name of Jesus.

5. By the power in the name of Jesus, I shall not succumb to any disease of the mind but I shall be of sound mind throughout this day, in the name of Jesus.

6. Any disease unto death that is common in my family, hear me and hear me well, I am not your candidate.

Therefore, I break off your hooks from my life now and I cut off your supply into my life. You shall not harm me, in the name of Jesus.

7. Father, protect me completely from any disease or infirmity that can pull down my business, in the name of Jesus.

8. I decree, according to the word of the Lord, I shall not die but live to declare what God has done in my life. As I step out of my house today, I will return to it safe, sound and better than when I left in the morning, in the name of Jesus.

*If you have the need and time, feel free to add more prayers at this point.*

# 13

# PRAYERS FOR THE EXPRESSION OF CHARACTER / PERSONALITY THAT WILL HONOR GOD

1. O Lord God of heaven, my life is available for you today. Convert my life into talking and walking epistles that will draw people unto you, in the name of Jesus.

2. My Father, install in me the filter of the Holy Ghost. Let everything I do today honor you, in the name of Jesus.

3. My Father, let the filter of the Holy Ghost purge all the words I shall speak today, in the name of Jesus.

4. Almighty God, give me the fortitude to remove any element of my character and lifestyle that is not pleasing to you, in the name of Jesus.

5. Lord Jesus, use my character as an agent to cause all men to be at peace with me and to favor me, in the name of Jesus.

# 14

# PRAYERS FOR PRODUCT-BASED BUSINESS OWNERS

## PRAYERS FOR YOUR PRODUCTS, CUSTOMERS & MARKETING

1. O great and awesome God, today I ask that you use my business as an example to demonstrate your power of favor in the life of a man, in the name of Jesus.

2. Heavenly Father, inspire me to create or stock products that people have been looking for so that they will be fall over themselves to patronize me, in the name of Jesus.

3. Almighty God, this morning I ask that you put your blessing upon all my products so that I can profit tremedously, in the name of Jesus.

4. O Lord my God, give me favor before customers so that they will be magnetized to my business, in the name of Jesus.

5. Father, as I open my doors today for business, let customers begin to stream in and make purchases, in the name of Jesus.

6. Today, I decree favor upon my products that are on the shelves of the stores and malls of my distributors, let people locate them, fall in love with them and buy them, in the name of Jesus.

7. Any spirit of rejection based on lack of familiarity with my product or for whatever reason, I come against you and I command you to depart from my life in the name of Jesus. My products will sell, sell, sell, in the name of Jesus.

8. I declare that wherever I go with my products today, doors will open unto me. I will breakthrough in life and business and I shall prosper, in the mighty name of Jesus.

9. Almighty God, make my customers become fanatic about and obsessed with my products. Cause them to help me market my business by spreading the word about the quality of my products to people they know and those that they do not know, in the name of Jesus.

10. O Lord, whenever people see my advertisements made through any medium, cause them to respond to the ads and convert them to passionate customers and fans of my business, in the name of Jesus.

## PRAYERS FOR EMPLOYEES AND BUSINESS PREMISES

1. O Lord, I pray, make me a true leader. Empower me with the ability to lead my workforce without fault, in the name of Jesus.

2. Heavenly Father, inspire my loyal, skilled and experienced employees to remain with me so that my business can be stable, in the name of Jesus.

3. Most High God, I ask that you send talented employees my way whose skills can help me grow my business, in the name of Jesus.

4. Lord, let my employees be devoted to my business and give their best while they are in my employ, in the name of Jesus.

5. Heavenly Father, open my eyes to identify and recognize employees who are giving their very best so that I can reward them accordingly in the name of Jesus.

6. Any agent of darkness that has infiltrated my company disguised as an employee, be revealed and be removed in the name of Jesus.

7. I decree this morning that my business will not suffer from arson committed by any digruntled employee, in the name of Jesus.

8. Again, this morning I decree that my business will not suffer from malicious theft committed by any digruntled employee, in the name of Jesus.

9. I cover my business premises in the blood of Jesus. It shall not burn to the ground, neither shall it be a candidate of looting or any other event of misfortune, in the name of Jesus.

10. O God, enlarge the coast of my business so that I can expand my present business location or relocate to a larger one, in the name of Jesus.

## PRAYERS TO ADDRESS REGULATORS AND COMPETITORS

1. Almighty God, let me always meet and exceed the standards set by the government regulator of my business, in the name of Jesus.

2. Lord, whenever I am asked to submit my products to the regulator in charge of my industry for any reason, give me favor. Let my products meet and exceed all standards set by the regulator, in the name of Jesus.

3. Heavenly Father, let any official working with the regulator and illegally demanding bribes, money or other favors from me be revealed and removed, in the name of Jesus.

4. Lord, show me the strategies of my competitors in the marketplace so that I can use my knowledge of these strategies to surpass them, in the name of Jesus.

5. My Father and my God, help me to out-innovate all my competitors in every way, in the name of Jesus.

6. I automatically convert any negativity thrown my way by detractors, competitors and all others into motivational vitamins with which to advance the cause of my business, in the name of Jesus.

7. By the power in the blood of Jesus, I frustrate the efforts of any evil competitor that wants my business to die so that his or hers can prosper. Their efforts shall not prosper against me in the name of Jesus.

8. O Lord, anoint me with the oil of gladness above my fellows. In every marketplace and industry in which I operate I shall succeed far and above all my competitors because the Almighty God is with me, in the name of Jesus.

## PRAYERS AGAINST NEGATIVE SPIRITUAL FORCES

1. I frustrate any attack of the devil on my business, in the name of Jesus.

2. I establish a defensive shield over my life and my family. Let any wicked spiritual arrow fired against my life, my family and my business return to sender in the name of Jesus.

3. I reject any satanically inspired spirit of discouragement. I refuse to be discouraged. Instead, I shall continue to work harder and prosper, in the name of Jesus.

4. Any power of darkness that has sworn that it is over their dead body that I shall prosper in business, Lord, do as they say, answer their prayers and let me prosper in the name of Jesus.

5. By the power in the blood of Jesus, I break any evil curse of darkness that has been issued against my business. Let the reverse of that curse manifest in my life in the name of Jesus.

6. Any man or woman that has been hired to curse my business for any reason, hear me and hear me well, as with the example of Balaam, the Almighty will convert all your curses into blessings for my favor, in the name of Jesus.

7. Any demonic physical object that has been dropped at my place of business in order to attack me or my business, I decree in the name of Jesus, you physical object of darkness, lose your power, in the name of Jesus.

8. Any sickness fashioned against me by powers of darkness, you shall not prosper, in the name of Jesus. I will not fall sick and my business will not suffer, in the name of Jesus.

9. Any sickness fashioned against members of my family with the purpose of making me spend all my resources and to kill my business, listen up, you shall not prosper in the name of Jesus. No member of my family shall fall victim to demonic sicknesses in the name of Jesus.

10. All arrows of loss, i fire them back to their senders in the name of Jesus.

11. All arrows of backwardness, I send them back to their senders, in the name of Jesus.

12. I decree that it is well with me, with my family members, with my employees and colleagues and with my business. I receive the power to make wealth. I shall prosper and I shall fulfill my destiny. It is well with me, in the mighty name of Jesus.

# 15

# PRAYERS FOR SERVICE-BASED BUSINESS OWNERS

## PRAYERS FOR YOUR SERVICE, CUSTOMERS & MARKETING

1. O great and awesome God, today I ask that you use my business as an example to demonstrate your power of favor in the life of a human being, in the name of Jesus.

2. Heavenly Father, inspire me to provide services that people have been looking for so that they will be fall over themselves to patronize me, in the name of Jesus.

3. Almighty God, this morning I ask that you put your blessing upon all the services that I render so that I can profit tremedously, in the name of Jesus.

4. O Lord my God, give me favor before customers so that they will be magnetized to my business, in the name of Jesus.

5. Father, as I open my doors today for business, let customers begin to stream in to use my services, in the name of Jesus.

7. Any spirit of rejection based on lack of familiarity with my services or for whatever reason, I come against you and I command you to depart from my life in the name of Jesus. My services will sell, sell, sell, in the name of Jesus.

8. I declare that wherever I go today, doors will open unto me. People will demand for my services. I will breakthrough in life and business and I shall prosper, in the mighty name of Jesus.

9. Almighty God, make my customers become fanatic about and obsessed with my services. Cause them to help me market my business by spreading the word about the quality of my services to people they know and those that they do not know, in the name of Jesus.

10. O Lord, whenever people see my advertisements made through any medium, cause them to respond to the ads and convert them to passionate customers and fans of my business, in the name of Jesus.

## PRAYERS FOR EMPLOYEES AND BUSINESS PREMISES

1. O Lord, I pray, make me a true leader. Empower me with the ability to lead my workforce without fault, in the name of Jesus.

2. Heavenly Father, inspire my loyal, skilled and experienced employees to remain with me so that my business can be stable, in the name of Jesus.

3. Most High God, I ask that you send talented employees my way whose skills can help me grow my business, in the name of Jesus.

4. Lord, let my employees be devoted to my business and give their best while they are in my employ, in the name of Jesus.

5. Heavenly Father, open my eyes to identify and recognize employees who are giving their very best so that I can reward them accordingly in the name of Jesus.

6. Any agent of darkness that has infiltrated my company disguised as an employee, be revealed and be removed in the name of Jesus.

7. I decree this morning that my business will not suffer from arson committed by any digruntled employee, in the name of Jesus.

8. Again, this morning I decree that my business will not suffer from malicious theft committed by any digruntled employee, in the name of Jesus.

9. I cover my business premises in the blood of Jesus. It shall not burn to the ground, neither shall it be a candidate of looting or any other event of misfortune, in the name of Jesus.

10. O God, enlarge the coast of my business so that I can expand my present business location or relocate to a larger one, in the name of Jesus.

## PRAYERS TO ADDRESS REGULATORS AND COMPETITORS

1. Almighty God, let me always meet and exceed the standards set by the government regulator of my business, in the name of Jesus.

2. Lord, whenever I am asked to submit my products to the regulator in charge of my industry for any reason, give me favor. Let my premises and my services meet and exceed all standards set by the regulator, in the name of Jesus.

3. Heavenly Father, let any official working with the regulator and illegally demanding bribes, money or other favors from me be revealed and removed, in the name of Jesus.

4. Lord, show me the strategies of my competitors in the marketplace so that I can use my knowledge of these strategies to surpass them, in the name of Jesus.

5. My Father and my God, help me to out-innovate all my competitors in every way, in the name of Jesus.

6. I automatically convert any negativity thrown my way by detractors, competitors and all others into motivational vitamins with which to advance the cause of my business, in the name of Jesus.

7. By the power in the blood of Jesus, I frustrate the efforts of any evil competitor that wants my business to die so that his or hers can prosper. Their efforts shall not prosper against me in the name of Jesus.

8. O Lord, anoint me with the oil of gladness above my fellows. In every marketplace and industry in which I operate I shall succeed far and above all my competitors because the Almighty God is with me, in the name of Jesus.

## PRAYERS AGAINST NEGATIVE SPIRITUAL FORCES

1. I frustrate any attack of the devil on my business, in the name of Jesus.

2. I establish a defensive shield over my life and my family. Let any wicked spiritual arrow fired against my life, my family and my business return to sender in the name of Jesus.

3. I reject any satanically inspired spirit of discouragement. I refuse to be discouraged. Instead, I shall continue to work harder and prosper, in the name of Jesus.

4. Any power of darkness that has sworn that it is over their dead body that I shall prosper in business, Lord, do as they say, answer their prayers and let me prosper in the name of Jesus.

5. By the power in the blood of Jesus, I break any evil curse of darkness that has been issued against my business. Let the reverse of that curse manifest in my life in the name of Jesus.

6. Any man or woman that has been hired to curse my business for any reason, hear me and hear me well, as with the example of Balaam, the Almighty will convert all your curses into blessings for my favor, in the name of Jesus.

7. Any demonic physical object that has been dropped at my place of business in order to attack me or my business, I decree in the name of Jesus, you physical object of darkness, lose your power, in the name of Jesus.

8. Any sickness fashioned against me by powers of darkness, you shall not prosper, in the name of Jesus. I will not fall sick and my business will not suffer, in the name of Jesus.

9. Any sickness fashioned against members of my family with the purpose of making me spend all my resources and to kill my business, listen up, you shall not prosper in the name of Jesus. No member of my family shall fall victim to demonic sicknesses in the name of Jesus.

10. All arrows of loss, i fire them back to their senders in the name of Jesus.

11. All arrows of backwardness, I send them back to their senders, in the name of Jesus.

12. I decree that it is well with me, with my family members, with my employees and colleagues and with my business. I receive the power to make wealth. I shall prosper and I shall fulfill my destiny. It is well with me, in the mighty name of Jesus.

# SECTION 3

# THE BLESSING

# 16

# THE BLESSING

**Now, finally, before you step out, place your right hand on your chest as you read out these words of blessings upon your life. Say amen at the end of each paragraph.**

As you go out today, may the Lord bless you and keep you.

May the Lord cause His face to shine upon you and be gracious unto you. He will give you peace and no weapon formed against you shall prosper. Every tongue that shall rise against you in judgment God will condemn. Whatsoever you lay your hands on today shall prosper. I decree upon your life that you shall eat the good of your city, state, country and this world and you shall not suffer any loss.

I pray that God will set you high above all nations of the earth. He will open the floodgates of heaven and pour out such blessing upon your life that there will not be room enough to store it. He will give you the desire of your heart and make all your plans succeed.

I decree unto your life today that you will be like a tree planted by the riverside. Your leaves will always be green. Even in the time of drought you will never cease to bear fruit.

I pray that God's blessing will be on your food and water and that He will take away sickness from you and your family. He will meet all your needs according to the riches of His glory in Christ Jesus.

According to the word of the Lord, blessed shall you be when you come in, and blessed shall you be when you go out. The Lord will cause your enemies who rise against you to be defeated before your face. They shall come out against you one way and flee before you seven ways. The Lord will command the blessing on you in your storehouses and in all to which you set your hand.

The Lord will grant you plenty of goods and make you wealthy. He will open to you His good treasure, the heavens, to give the rain to your land in its season, and to bless all the work of your hand again and again. You shall lend to people but you shall never borrow from anyone.

The Lord will make you the head and not the tail. You shall be above only, and not be beneath even as you obey the commandments of the Lord your God, in Jesus name, Amen.

**Take charge of this day! God bless you.**

Printed in Great Britain
by Amazon